THE SECRET TO MONTHLY
INCOME FOR LIFE

RON GROENKE
TRADING TECHNOLOGY EXPERT

ISBN: 9781726674263

 wallstreetwinning.com

You've made a great decision.

Options are a mathematics and probability game.
Having an advantage over other
traders is how you win in the market.

The purpose of this book is to help you understand
how options can work for you so you can start making monthly
income for life with trade data that can immediately put the odds
in your favor.

But… let's not ignore the elephant in the room.

Investing is a contact sport. It involves risk of loss and is
certainly not suitable for everyone. No matter how much you
"know" or don't know, the markets can serve you a big pile of
losses out of nowhere.
So be smart and don't trade with money you can't afford to lose.

Do you know who practices this better than anyone….

Yup, " Wall Street Winning."

One of the biggest reasons why "Winning" investors get richer
is that they have access to the right math and data . In other
words, they are right more often then wrong, have a higher win
rate, and for a longer period of time, than you.

Let's see if we can't level the field a little bit and share with you
what these investors know that make them "Wall Street
Winners."

Trading stocks, futures, and options involves substantial risk of loss and is not suitable for
everyone. Past performance is not necessarily indicative of futures results. Options selling may
involve unlimited losses.

Truth # 1

Options were designed to expire worthless!

According to the CME Group (one of the largest options exchanges in world), nearly 70+% of options expire worthless.

Yes, nearly 70+%...
If this comes as a surprise to you, then you're in the right place.

The reason why so many options expire worthless is as simple as it gets. They were designed to do so.

But... let's not ignore the elephant in the room.

Options were created to be an insurance product for stock and commodity investors. Therefore, just like all insurance products, option contracts have an expiration date. If options are like insurance contracts, would you rather be the person buying the contract or selling the contract?

Hint: Insurance companies have mushroomed
to multi-trillion dollar businesses.

"Wall Street Winners" have known this since the 80's and have been positioning themselves to take advantage of this little known fact ever since.

This information is the foundation of the "Wall Street Winning" "Done for You" system. Let's take this concept a step further.

Trading stocks, futures, and options involves substantial risk of loss and is not suitable for everyone. Past performance is not necessarily indicative of futures results. Options selling may involve unlimited losses.

During weekly options contracts, a lot can happen. The price or value of the stock can fluctuate wildly. If you were the buyer of the contract, you could make big money one minute or have a worthless option the next.

The most crucial factor with options is timing.

Why?

It's about math. The way an option contract functions is that the underlying asset needs to be at a set price by a certain period of time or the option becomes worthless. So, think about it. If you BUY an option and in order for you to make a profit the stock or futures contract needs to move say 20% in 5 days, what do you think your odds are? Probably not great.

Now what do you think happens to the options contract you bought? Yeah… it becomes worth a lot less when you try to sell it.

In a nutshell, you make money by selling options.

I'm sure you have heard options are risky.
Remember, options are a zero sum game. So if someone is losing money on these types of trades, there is another person profiting from them.

OK, now its time for you to start being a "Wall Street Winner."

Trading stocks, futures, and options involves substantial risk of loss and is not suitable for everyone. Past performance is not necessarily indicative of futures results. Options selling may involve unlimited losses.

WALL STREET WINNING

You now know two major pieces of information:

Nearly 70+% of all

options expire worthless

- & -

You make money with

options by SELLING

Let's apply them to some real options strategies.

RON GROENKE
TRADING TECHNOLOGY EXPERT

The first thing you need to start doing is sell instead of buying - collect money instead of parting with it.

By doing this, you immediately become the house. Sellers have the odds in their favor. Remember options expire 70+% of the time.

What if you had a tool to increase your win rate to over 90%. Do you think this would give you an advantage over the average investor? I think YES.

When choosing to sell a call option you are agreeing to forego the unlimited upside potential.

Why? Because we would rather have the odds in our favor and take the guarantee to the bank.
As the old expression goes...

"It's better to have one bird in the hand, than two in the bush."

"Wall Street Winning" does not only believe this, but we purposely avoid swinging for the fences. We only go for singles and doubles, because that is what wins the game.

Buying options is like going for a home run at every bat. The odds of you striking out go up each time you approach the batters box.

This is not the mindset of a "Wall Street Winner."

Winners are all about consistency.

Trading stocks, futures, and options involves substantial risk of loss and is not suitable for everyone. Past performance is not necessarily indicative of futures results. Options selling may involve unlimited losses.

Another thing to consider is the risk of loss. When we sell options "naked," then we technically have some risk.

Yes, even with a 90+% win rate there is risk.

How is this possible?

Again, this is simple. Remember that if you are the option seller, then you become the house. So if the other trader on the opposite side of your trade is right and the market moves in his or her favor, you need to buy the stock on which you sold a Put Option but at a lower price.

So to trade like a "Winner" you need to play the long game, which is to keep selling options and taking advantage of the fact that potentially the majority of them it will work out in your favor.

Our data has a win rate of 97% and stock is put to us less than 14% of the time.

The good news is even when we sell "naked puts" we are only selling these puts on stocks with good fundamentals that we do not mind owning. The best part is if this happens we get them at a lower price.

Trading stocks, futures, and options involves substantial risk of loss and is not suitable for everyone. Past performance is not necessarily indicative of futures results. Options selling may involve unlimited losses.

Are Options Risky?

NO - Not at all. In fact, with the right system and the right data we will show you how you limit your downside risk, while keeping the odds in your favor, and have a dependable source of monthly income.

We will get to this in a minute.

Most traders think that they have to "know" where the market is going to make money trading. This is sort of a half-truth.

"Wall Street Winners" don't always need to know where the market is going at all times. Instead, they just need to know where the market is most likely not going to go.

Take for example your favorite stock or ETF. Knowing for sure where the price will be for that asset in a particular period of time is virtually impossible to forecast. Yet, that's what every investor tries to do everyday.

If I asked you where you thought the prices would probably NOT go in the same period of time, you might feel a lot more confident about that answer.

This is what the "Wall Street Winning" options data does. We look at asset fundamentals and ask what is the probability of this asset getting to this price or that price in "x" number of days.

Next, we look at the premium for those options and determine if the return of that option is worth it. If it is overvalued and the odds of the underlying asset reaching that price is low, we will consider selling that option.

This strategy is the opposite of the hope and pray technique used by most investors. The options seller is simply waiting for the market to do it's thing and as long as the price doesn't move too fast towards the options they sold, we are in good shape.

All we have to do is just wait for the options to be worth less then what we sold it for. Pretty cool right?

Trading stocks, futures, and options involves substantial risk of loss and is not suitable for everyone. Past performance is not necessarily indicative of futures results. Options selling may involve unlimited losses.

Wall Street Winners have also figured out a way to collect money every time they place a trade.

Most options traders buy options and therefore have to debit their trading accounts every time they place a trade. They only get their money back when they sell the equity, hopefully, a profit.

The winning options traders sell options so they can collect "income" called premium. Again, think of the house in Vegas. Every time a sucker places a bet, the house gets its money first.

Same goes for the options seller. This is a nice perk and a welcomed change for many investors.

Here's how it works:

The options seller sells an option to a buyer. The buyer's investment goes directly into the seller's account. The option seller holds the money in their account until either a buyer exits the position, exercises the option, or the option expires worthless.
The latter of these three conditions is what the options seller is hoping for.

If the option expires worthless, then the option seller gets to keep all the money collected minus commissions and fees.

However, even though the money goes into the seller's account, it's technically not the seller's money until the trade is complete.

One last perk for the options seller... they can buy the option back at any time. This is a huge plus!

Trading stocks, futures, and options involves substantial risk of loss and is not suitable for everyone. Past performance is not necessarily indicative of futures results. Options selling may involve unlimited losses.

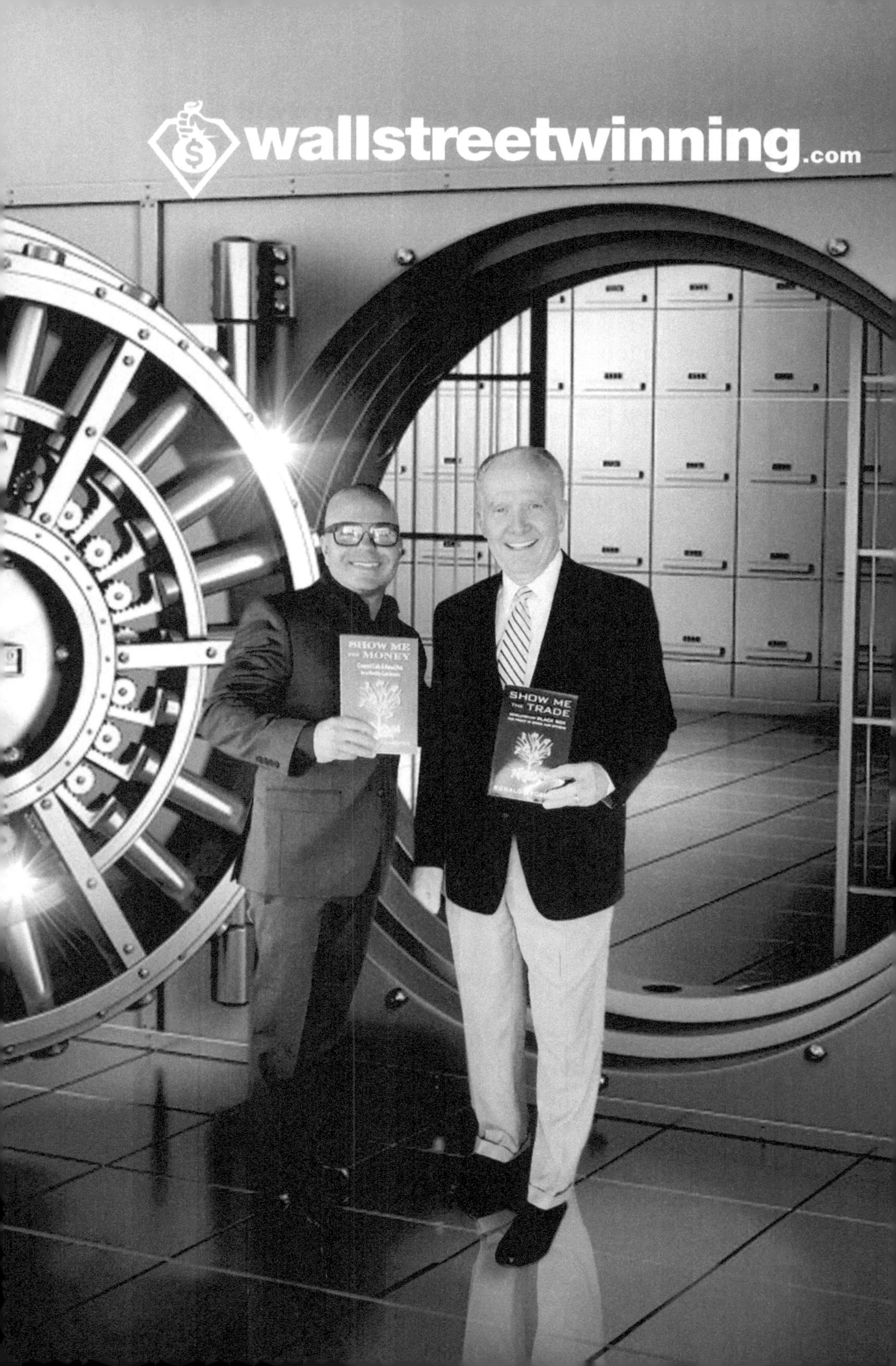
wallstreetwinning.com
SHOW ME THE MONEY
SHOW ME THE TRADE

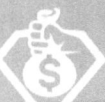

Income For Life Strategy

There is one primary strategy we implement involving the selling of options.
(The Double Up)

wallstreetwinning.com

COVERED CALL

Covered Call, or Call writing, involves buying the underlying equity and selling a call option.

A covered call writer has a neutral to bearish view of a market.

The best return is achieved when selling slightly out-of-the-money options.

This means selling a call with a strike price that is above the equity price or selling a put with a strike price below the equity price. In either case a dollar amount, or premium, is collected and credited to a client's account.

In the case of a short call this premium is retained if, by expiration, the equity price has moved lower, stayed the same, or moved higher but not up to the strike price of the call.

Learn how you can use this technique on your own investing today. Join us for a free training @ www.wallstreetwinning.com

---

Trading stocks, futures, and options involves substantial risk of loss and is not suitable for everyone. Past performance is not necessarily indicative of futures results. Options selling may involve unlimited losses.

THE NAKED PUT

A Naked Put is a strategy in which a trader or options writer has a neutral to bullish view on a market.

A **Put Option** is a contract that gives the holder the right (but not the obligation) to sell a specific stock at a predetermined price on or before a certain date (called the expiration date).

In the case of a short put the premium is retained if the equity has moved higher, stayed the same, or moved lower, but not down to the strike price of the put.

This is the WINNINGEST options strategy for trading in all markets.

Learn how you can use this technique on your own investing today. Join us for a free training @ www.wallstreetwinning.com

Trading stocks, futures, and options involves substantial risk of loss and is not suitable for everyone. Past performance is not necessarily indicative of futures results. Options selling may involve unlimited losses.

DOUBLE UP
(Income For Life Strategy)

This strategy is a combination of a covered call and a naked put. It provides an excellent way to generate income on a continuous basis

This is the underlying strategy of the Done For You investing system. This is where weekly trade setups are published providing excellent returns with follow-up steps along the way for weekly income.

This strategy can be repeated over and over when a stock or ETF trades in a channel or small range. For example, buy at $15.50, sell a call at $16, and a put at $15. If the stock does not move much you continue with a new call and put in the channel range. If the stock moves up, you implement a call and put in the new range. If the stock moves down, you usually can sell calls at the lower strike price (at or above break even) and still generate an acceptable return. This gives you a positive return on the investment even when the price of the stock goes down.

> Learn how you can use this technique on your own investing today. Join us for a free training @ www.wallstreetwinning.com.

Trading stocks, futures, and options involves substantial risk of loss and is not suitable for everyone. Past performance is not necessarily indicative of futures results. Options selling may involve unlimited losses.

DONE FOR YOU

The best way to demonstrate any strategy or algorithm is to publish the results. Click here to see our RESULTS.

The Done For You trade setups from our trade technology have produced a 95% win rate. Every trade has been published (good and bad). The trade setup uses an investment value as close to $10,000 as possible. This can be allocated as desired. Since one option contract controls 100 shares, rounded lots of 100 shares are used in all of the examples.

The Done For You Plus (data) provides three opportunities each week and six in the Pro package . The performance is updated each week based on the results of the current week setup. New sets up are published each weekend prior to market open.

The "Trading Room Live" is a twice weekly video training session where you can watch an experienced trader make the modeled trades with full management expertise. For those who qualify for the program it provides accountably and the ability to get reproducible results in your account if you take action.

Learn how you can use this technique on your own investing today. Join us for a free training @ www.wallstreetwinning.com

---

Trading stocks, futures, and options involves substantial risk of loss and is not suitable for everyone. Past performance is not necessarily indicative of futures results. Options selling may involve unlimited losses.

RESULTS

Wall Street Winning has earned its niche as the premier options trade data publisher. The bulk of our clients participate in the many advantages options income provide. Options are a more conservative, lower risk strategy for consistent monthly income.

Basic Plan Results
2016 Win Rate 96% Avg Weekly Return 1.37% Avg Hold Time 13.76 Days Put Assignment Rate 18%
2017 Win Rate 97% Avg Weekly Return 1.09% Avg Hold Time 13.12 Days Put Assignment Rate 6%
2018 YTD Win Rate 100% Avg Weekly Return 1.49% Avg Hold Time 11.06 Days Put Assignment Rate 0%

Plus Plan Results
2016 Win Rate 95% Avg Weekly Return 1.34% Avg Hold Time 15.93 Days Put Assignment Rate 18%
2017 Win Rate 97% Avg Weekly Return .91% Avg Hold Time 19.18 Days Put Assignment Rate 6%
2018 YTD Win Rate 95% Avg Weekly Return 1.45% Avg Hold Time 12.75 Days Put Assignment Rate 0%

The Income For Life strategy enables you to compound and grow your nest egg or even trade simply for income. It beats real estate or any other investment vehicle we know of.

Learn how you can use this technique on your own investing today. Join us for a free training @ www.wallstreetwinning.com

Trading stocks, futures, and options involves substantial risk of loss and is not suitable for everyone. Past performance is not necessarily indicative of futures results. Options selling may involve unlimited losses.

How is this all possible? It sounds too good to be true.

There have been many questions on "how is it possible" that the **"Done For You"** trade setups are as successful as published. It is all about the math and data being sorted, filtered, and processed each and every day.

Determining the WHAT and the WHEN is a big task.

Mining for Options is even bigger.

	STRIKE DATE	STRIKE PRICE	TYPE	BID/ASK MIDPOINT	DAYS TO EXP	30 DAY RETURN IF		RISK REWARD
CYBR OPTIONS INCOME STRATEGY			PRICE 49.95		DAYS OUT > 1		RECALCULATE	
COVERED CALL	07-07-17	49.50	ITM	1.15	7	SOLD 6.01%	EXP. 9.87%	6.6
COVERED CALL	07-07-17	50.00	ATM	0.70	7	SOLD 6.44%	EXP. 6.01%	6.1
COVERED CALL	07-07-17	50.50	OTM	0.68	7	SOLD 10.51%	EXP. 5.79%	6.5
NAKED PUT	07-07-17	49.00	OTM	0.78	7		EXP. 6.78%	6.7
NAKED PUT	07-07-17	49.50	ATM	0.75	7		EXP. 6.49%	5.5
NAKED PUT	07-07-17	50.00	ITM	0.63	7		EXP. 4.93%	0.8

Trading stocks, futures, and options involves substantial risk of loss and is not suitable for everyone. Past performance is not necessarily indicative of futures results. Options selling may involve unlimited losses.

All of the data and strategies featured in this book are available at:
www.wallstreetwinning.com

Yikes, there's risk!

Trading stocks, commodity futures and options on stocks or commodities carries risk, period.

You can limit risk when purchasing options, but if you continue to lose premium on a continuous basis, your losses will accumulate. A short option can carry the same risk as a futures contract; therefore there is a margin requirement. If the market moves against your short option position, your margin can never be (more than the underlying futures contract)might increase and you may owe substantial additional capital without much warning in order to simply maintain your position.

There is substantial risk of loss in options futures trading. Only risk capital should be used.

We will work with you to determine what risk parameters and particular selling strategies are right for you.
Even though we believe selling options is more favorable than buying options, the biggest advantage to you is that selling options gives you a larger margin for error. Selling out-of-the-money options allows you to profit from sideways markets, trending markets, and at times profit can occur even if the underlying market moves against the sellers position!

Trading stocks, futures, and options involves substantial risk of loss and is not suitable for everyone. Past performance is not necessarily indicative of futures results. Options selling may involve unlimited losses.

Wall Street Winning
Please visit wallstreetwinning.com take our free training
then book a qualifying call regarding this program
or any other needs you may have.
Fully Managed Wealth Management products are
also available for accredited investors.

TRADING FUTURES AND OPTIONS INVOLVES RISK AND ONLY RISK CAPITAL
SHOULD BEUSED. COLLECTION OF PREMIUM DOES NOT MEAN RETENTION
OF PREMIUM.

www.ingramcontent.com/pod-product-compliance
Lightning Source LLC
Chambersburg PA
CBHW031600210526
45464CB00003B/1367